Next Time You See a
SPIDERWEB

BY EMILY MORGAN

NSTA Kids
National Science Teachers Association
Arlington, Virginia

National Science Teachers Association

Claire Reinburg, Director
Wendy Rubin, Managing Editor
Amanda O'Brien, Associate Editor
Donna Yudkin, Book Acquisitions Coordinator

ART AND DESIGN
Will Thomas Jr., Director

Cover photo by Judd Patterson

PRINTING AND PRODUCTION
Catherine Lorrain, Director

NATIONAL SCIENCE TEACHERS ASSOCIATION
David L. Evans, Executive Director
David Beacom, Publisher

1840 Wilson Blvd., Arlington, VA 22201
www.nsta.org/store
For customer service inquiries, please call 800-277-5300.

Lexile® measure: 1080L

Library of Congress Cataloging-in-Publication Data

Morgan, Emily R. (Emily Rachel), 1973- author.
 Next time you see a spiderweb / by Emily Morgan.
    pages cm -- (Next time you see)
 Audience: K to grade 3.
 Summary: "If you know children who say "Ick!" when they spot a spider, this book will make them say "Ooh!" instead. Next Time You See a Spiderweb describes how these skilled creatures weave nature's most clever traps--their webs. It shows how spiders snare their prey with messy tangled webs and intricate orb webs. Readers will learn how spiders spin sticky silk without getting stuck themselves."-- Provided by publisher.
 Includes bibliographical references.
 ISBN 978-1-938946-34-9 (print) -- ISBN 978-1-941316-31-3 (library) -- ISBN 978-1-941316-40-5 (e-book) 1. Spiders--Juvenile literature. 2. Spider webs--Juvenile literature. I. Title.
 QL458.4.M635 2015
 595.4'4--dc23
                          2015030184

Cataloging-in-Publication Data for the e-book are available from the Library of Congress.
e-LCCN: 2015034405

Library binding ISBN: 978-1-941316-31-3

To Mr. Gary Courts, my high school biology teacher, for nurturing my love of science and supporting my work all these years later.

"... the web itself is a miracle."
—E. B. White,
Charlotte's Web

A Note to Parents and Teachers

The books in this series are intended to be read with a child *after* she has had some experience with the featured objects or phenomena. For example, take a walk in a park or natural area and look for spiderwebs. Notice the size, location, and patterns of the webs. Take photos of the various webs and compare them. Talk about what you observe and what you wonder.

Then, after you have had some experiences observing these fascinating structures, read this book together. Take time to pause and share your learnings and wonderings with each other. You will find that new learnings often lead to more questions.

The *Next Time You See* books are not meant to present facts to be memorized. They are written to inspire a sense of wonder about nature and foster a desire to learn more about the natural world. Children are naturally fascinated by spiderwebs, and when they learn that these webs are clever traps made by small and skillful spiders that never had a single lesson, these structures become even more remarkable. My wish is that after reading this book, you and your child feel a sense of wonder the next time you see a spiderweb.

—Emily Morgan

Next time you see a spiderweb, take a few moments to observe it carefully.

Do you see a pattern to the web, or does it look like a tangled mess?

Follow the lines at the edges of the web. Can you figure out what they are attached to?

Do you see a spider on the web?

Is there anything trapped in the web?

Gently touch the outer edge of the web. How does it feel? How does it move when you tap it with your finger?

Spiderwebs are some of the most fascinating structures in nature. You can find them in many places and in different shapes and sizes. Some have elegant patterns, and others look like a jumble of threads. Have you ever wondered why spiders make webs?

Food! Spiderwebs are traps designed to catch food for spiders to eat. Spiders eat other animals, mostly insects and other small invertebrates. Web-building spiders catch their prey in many ways, using different types of webs.

You've probably seen a spiderweb that looks like a mess of threads. These are known as *tangled webs* or *cobwebs*. When an insect flies into or walks over this kind of web, it becomes entangled in the silk threads, making it easy for the spider to catch the insect.

You may have noticed a web that lies flat across the grass or on a bush. These webs are called *sheet webs*. The spider creates a sheet of silk and weaves special strands above it. When an insect flies into the top threads, it gets knocked down and captured in the sheet below.

Another interesting kind of web is a *funnel-web*. These webs are wide at the top and get smaller at the base. The spider hides inside the funnel and waits. When it feels an insect walking across the web, the spider rushes across the web and grabs its prey.

Perhaps the most well-known type of spiderweb is the *orb web*. These beautiful and elaborate webs look like the wheel of a bicycle, with threads connecting each spoke. When an insect flies into the web, it becomes trapped in sticky silk. The spider, usually waiting in the center of the web or hiding nearby, feels the vibration on the threads and rushes in to get its prey.

A spiderweb is a marvelous trap because it gives the spider the ability to sense an area much larger than itself. A spider can feel vibrations through the silk and knows exactly when and where something touches its web. Just think: With its web, an orb-weaving spider that might be the size of a dime has the ability to sense an area larger than a dinner plate.

If you have ever accidentally walked through a spiderweb, you probably found it difficult to get the web off of you. This is because many spiderwebs are sticky. However, spiders are able to move around in their webs quickly and easily without getting stuck. Have you ever wondered why spiders don't get trapped in their own webs?

There are several reasons why spiders don't get caught in their own traps. One reason is that not all spider silk is sticky. Orb-weaving spiders appear to know which parts of their webs are sticky and which parts are not, and they tend to avoid the sticky parts. Another reason is that spiders have tiny structures on the ends of their legs that reduce their contact with the silk. Finally, some spiders actually have a nonstick coating on their legs that keeps them from sticking to the web.

Spider silk is made in silk glands inside the spider's body. The silk is liquid when it is in the silk glands and becomes solid as the spider pulls it out of its body through special structures called *spinnerets*. The spider pulls the silk out with its legs and can combine the thin strands that come out of its spinnerets to make different kinds of threads. Can you find the spider's spinnerets in this picture?

Spiders have an extraordinary ability to make different kinds of silk depending on the job they need to do. For example, an orb weaver uses strong, tight silk to build the frame and radial lines (spokes) of the web. Then, it uses a thinner, more elastic type of silk to make a spiral to connect the spokes. Finally, it creates a second spiral with sticky silk to trap the prey.

It is astonishing that these small creatures are able to make such elaborate and efficient traps without a single lesson! Spiders are born knowing how to build webs—they don't need anyone to teach them.

Not all spiders build webs. In fact, about half of spider species have other clever ways to catch food. For example, jumping spiders use their excellent vision to detect prey, and then they pounce on it.

Net-casting spiders hold a net of silk between their front legs. When their prey passes by, the spider sweeps it up in the net.

Fishing spiders wait on or near water, with their legs resting on the surface, and they attack prey when they feel vibrations on the water.

Trap-door spiders build a trap door over their burrow and attack when they feel something walk across it.

Even though not all spiders build webs, all spiders do produce silk. Most spiders use silk to make a *dragline*, a single thread they leave behind them when they walk or jump. This is a sort of safety line they can use to quickly climb back to where they started. Have you ever seen a single thread of spider silk shimmering in the sunlight? It was probably a dragline that a spider left behind.

Spiders also use silk to make other structures, such as egg sacs. Some species, like this jumping spider, even use silk to build a retreat that can serve as a hideout.

People have long been fascinated by the incredible strength and flexibility of spider silk. Some spider silk is stronger than a thread of steel, and some can stretch up to three times its length without breaking. Scientists are trying to mimic spider silk to create new materials that could be used for ultrastrong armor, bandages, ropes, parachutes, and lightweight clothing.

Engineers and architects are intrigued by the durability of spiderwebs. They have noticed that when a spiderweb is damaged, only part of it breaks, while the rest of it remains stable. Studying the construction of spiderwebs might help engineers and architects design structures that can withstand disasters such as earthquakes.

So, next time you see a spiderweb, remember that beautiful web is actually a brilliant trap. A small, skillful spider made an amazing material and wove it into that ingenious design to capture its food. Isn't that remarkable?

About the Photos

Touching a spiderweb
(Tom Uhlman)

A field of spiderwebs after a heavy dew
(Judd Patterson)

Spider with prey
(Steven David Johnson)

Observing a tangled web
(Clay Bolt)

Bowl and doily spider
(Tom Uhlman)

Funnel-web
(Clay Bolt)

Orb web
(Judd Patterson)

Orb web reflecting light
(Judd Patterson)

Touching a sticky web
(Tom Uhlman)

Spider on its web
(Judd Patterson)

Spider spinning silk
(Steven David Johnson)

Orb web between two flowers
(Steven David Johnson)

Orb web in the tall grass
(Judd Patterson)

Jumping spider with prey
(Nicky Bay)

Net-casting spider
(Nicky Bay)

Fishing spider
(Clay Bolt)

Trap-door spider
(Nicky Bay)

Spider leaving a dragline
(Steven David Johnson)

Jumping spider in a silk retreat
(Clay Bolt)

Spider on a thread in the sunlight
(Steven David Johnson)

Worn orb web
(Judd Patterson)

Observing an orb web
(Tom Uhlman)

Building a masking tape web
(Tom Uhlman)

31

ACTIVITIES TO ENCOURAGE A SENSE OF WONDER ABOUT SPIDERWEBS

❖ Go on a spiderweb hunt. Early morning is best because dew will make the spiderwebs easier to see. Print out the Spider Bingo sheet from the National Wildlife Federation (see Websites section below) and see if you can find all of the different types of webs.

❖ Take photographs of spiderwebs around your school or home. Compare the photos and note the similarities and differences between the webs.

❖ Watch a time-lapse video of a spider making an orb web on the Wonderopolis website (see Websites section).

❖ Make a model of a spiderweb in a door frame using masking tape. Create a frame and radial threads out of the nonsticky side and use the sticky side to add a capture spiral. Toss some wads of paper into the web to represent flying insects. Do they stick? How is your web similar to a real spiderweb? How is it different?

RESOURCES

Hillyard, P. 2011. *The private life of spiders*. Princeton, NJ: Princeton University Press.

Robertson, B. 2011. Science 101: Why don't spiders stick to their own webs? *Science & Children* 49 (1): 68–69.

WEBSITES

National Wildlife Federation: Observe Spider Webs With Spider Bingo
www.nwf.org/kids/family-fun/outdoor-activities/spider-bingo.aspx

Wonderopolis: Wonder of the Day # 120: Why Do Spiders Spin Webs?
http://wonderopolis.org/wonder/why-do-spiders-spin-webs

Next Time You See series
www.nexttimeyousee.com

Downloadable classroom activities can be found at *www.nsta.org/nexttime-spiderweb*.